1774

Felicity's Craft Book

*A Look at
Crafts from the
Past with Projects
You Can Make Today*

Pleasant Company Publications, Inc.

First Edition.
Printed in the United States of America.
94 95 96 97 98 99 WCR 10 9 8 7 6 5 4 3 2 1

The American Girls Collection® and Felicity Merriman® are
registered trademarks of Pleasant Company Incorporated.

PICTURE CREDITS
The following individuals and organizations have generously
given permission to reprint illustrations in this book:
Page 1—Colonial Williamsburg Foundation; 5—The Smithsonian Institution
(right); Taken from *Child Life in Colonial Days* by Alice Morse Earle, © 1961,
The Macmillan Company (left); 7—The Smithsonian Institution; 8—Rare Book
Department, Free Library of Philadelphia; 9—From the Collections of Henry Ford
Museum & Greenfield Village; 10—Taken from *Inkstands & Inkwells, A Collector's
Guide* by Betty and Ted Rivera, © 1973; 11—Courtesy, Winterthur Museum; 12, 13
(both images)—Colonial Williamsburg Foundation; 15—Detail of *La Primavera* (about
1478), an oil painting on wood panel by Sandro Botticelli, Uffizi Gallery, Florence, Italy
(SCALA/Art Resource); 19—West, Benjamin, *Benjamin Franklin Drawing Electricity
from the Sky*, Philadelphia Museum of Art: Mr. and Mrs. Wharton Sinkler Collection;
20—Courtesy of the Department of Special Collections, Memorial Library,
University of Wisconsin-Madison; 25—Taken from *Home Life in Colonial Days* by
Alice Morse Earle, © 1954, The Macmillan Company (top); M. and M. Karolik
Collection, Courtesy, Museum of Fine Arts, Boston (bottom); 27—Courtesy,
Winterthur Museum; 28—Taken from *Child Life in Colonial Days* by Alice Morse Earle,
© 1961, The Macmillan Company; 29—Gift of Mrs. Samuel Cabot, Courtesy, Museum
of Fine Arts, Boston (top); Shelburne Museum, Shelburne, Vermont, Photograph by
Ken Burris (bottom); 33—Taken from *Colonial Kitchens, Their Furnishings, and Their
Gardens* by Frances Phipps, © 1972, Hawthorn Books, Inc.; 36, 37 (right)—Colonial
Williamsburg Foundation; 37 (left)—New York Merchant Wm. Denning and Family,
Collection of Mr. & Mrs. W. Denning Harvey, Taken from *The American Heritage
History of the Thirteen Colonies*, 1967, American Heritage Publishing Co., Inc. (left);
38—Weidenfeld & Nicolson Archive; 41—Colonial Williamsburg Foundation.

Edited by Jodi Evert
Written by Rebecca Sample Bernstein and Jodi Evert
Designed and Art Directed by Jane S. Varda
Produced by Karen Bennett, Laura Paulini, and Pat Tuchscherer
Cover Illustration by Dan Andreasen
Inside Illustrations by Geri Strigenz Bourget
Photography by Mark Salisbury
Historical and Picture Research by Polly Athan,
Rebecca Sample Bernstein, Jodi Evert, and Doreen Smith
Crafts Made by Jean doPico and June Pratt
Craft Testing Coordinated by Jean doPico
Prop Research by Leslie Cakora

All the instructions in this book have been tested by both children and adults.
Results from their testing were incorporated into this book. Nonetheless, all
recommendations and suggestions are made without any guarantees on the part of
Pleasant Company Publications Incorporated. Because of differing tools, materials,
conditions, and individual skills, the publisher disclaims liability for any injuries,
losses, or other damages that may result from using the information in this book.

Library of Congress Cataloging-in-Publication Data

Felicity's craft book : a look at crafts from the past with projects you can make today.
— 1st ed.
p. cm.
ISBN 1-56247-121-X
1. Handicraft—Juvenile literature. 2. Handicraft—United States—Juvenile literature.
3. United States—Social life and customs—To 1775—Juvenile literature.
[1. Handicraft. 2. United States—Social life and customs—To 1775.]
TT160.F45 1994 745.5—dc20 94-3373 CIP

CONTENTS

Special thanks to all the children and adults who tested the crafts and gave us their valuable comments:

Stephanie Auen and her mother Carolyn Schoenwald

Hattie Bach and her mother Shannon Bach

Jessica Baumgarten and her mother Rose Baumgarten

Whitney Bembenek and her mother Debbi Bembenek

Jennifer Borgwardt and her mother Joanne Borgwardt

Nina Borokhim and her mother Barbara Borokhim

Alisa Brown and her mother Marlene Brown

Emily De Clercq and her mother Nancylee Bach

Anna Engelhart and her mother Teresa Engelhart

Laura Epstein and her mother Amy Epstein

Eryka Exum and her mother Laurie Exum

Sonya Frankowski and her mother Christine Frankowski

Alex Frey and his mother Mary Ellen Frey

Natalie Hegg and her mother Jill Hegg

Kari Jordan and her mother Karen Jordan

Tracy Juisto and her mother Jean Juisto

Taryn Knetter and her mother Traci Knetter

Nicole Kuehn and her mother Jill Kuehn

Cassie and Tory Lee and their mother Debra Lee

Laura Martin and her mother Denise Martin

Sarah Miller and her mother Ruth Miller

Mary Minahan and her mother Lisa Minahan

Emily Morrison and her mother Kim Morrison

Katie Moser and her mother Amy Moser

Meghan Moyer and her mother Deb Moyer

Jamie O'Connell and her mother Debbie O'Connell

Rebecca Paddock and her mother Susan Paddock

Jillian Parish and her mother Sally Parish

Cheryl Pederson and her mother Donna Pederson

Kati Peiss and her mother Kristi Peiss

Erica Perry and her mother Susan Perry

Sarah Peterson and her mother Nan Peterson

Allison Ridgely and her mother Carolyn Ridgely

Mollie Rostad and her mother Genie Campbell

Jessa Sharkey and her mother Paulette Sharkey

Erica and Kate Skog and their mother Judy Skog

Dina Sussman-Gaedke and her mother Nancy Gaedke

Heather Thue and her mother Jane Thue

Rachel Vitense and her mother Mary Vitense

Rachel Wiederhoeft and her mother Phyllis Wiederhoeft

CRAFTS FROM THE PAST

When English colonists first came to America, they got many of their supplies, such as dishes and tools, from England. Colonists didn't have much time to make those things for themselves. To survive, they needed to spend their time building homes and growing crops.

By Felicity's time, the colonies were more settled. Many families still lived on farms, but some families lived in cities like Williamsburg. Skilled women and men spun thread, wove cloth, sewed clothes, and crafted fine dishes and furniture. Some craftspeople taught teen-age *apprentices*. An apprentice agreed to work for a craftsperson for several years in exchange for learning the craft.

As the colonies became more independent, some colonists, called *Patriots*, wanted to be free from England. Colonists called *Loyalists* supported the king's rule. When the Patriots decided to fight for their freedom, the king stopped sending supplies to the colonies. That made it more important than ever for colonists to make things for themselves. Patriots worked together to make enough coats, shirts, shoes, and gunpowder for their soldiers.

FELICITY ❧ 1774

Felicity Merriman was a spritely, spunky colonial girl, growing up in Williamsburg, Virginia, in 1774. She grew up just as the United States of America was becoming a nation.

A young woman painting with watercolors in the mid-1700s.

Learning how and why crafts were made long ago will help you understand what it was like to grow up the way Felicity did. Making the crafts she might have made will bring history alive for you today.

CRAFT TIPS

This list of tips gives you some hints about creating the crafts in this book. But this is the most important tip: **work with an adult**. The best thing about these crafts is the fun you will have making them together.

1. Choose a time that suits you and the adult who's working with you, so that you will both enjoy making crafts together.

2. You can find most of the materials listed in this book in your home or at craft and fabric stores. If an item in the materials list is starred (*), look at the bottom of the list to find out where you can get it.

3. If you don't have something you need or can't find it at the store, think of something similar you could use. You might just think of something that works even better!

4. Read the instructions for a craft all the way through before you start it. Look at the pictures. They will help you understand the steps.

5. If there's a step that doesn't make sense to you, try it out with a piece of scrap paper or fabric first. Sometimes acting it out helps.

6. Select a good work area for your craft project. Pick a place that has plenty of light and is out of reach of pets and younger brothers and sisters.

PAINTS AND BRUSHES

*You'll use water-based, or **acrylic**, paints to make some of the crafts in this book. Here are a few hints for using paints and brushes:*

- *Don't dip your brush into the paint bottle. Squeeze a little paint onto newspaper or a paper plate.*

- *Have a bowl of water handy to clean the brush each time you change colors.*

- *Make sure one color is dry before adding another.*

- *Clean your brush with soap and water and let it dry before you put it away.*

7. Wear an apron, tie back your hair, and roll up your sleeves. Cover your work area with newspapers and gather all the materials you will need before you start.

8. It pays to be careful. Be sure to get an adult's help when the instructions tell you to. Have an adult help you use tools properly. Don't use the stove or oven without an adult's permission.

9. Pay attention when using sharp knives and scissors so you don't cut your fingers! Remember—good, sharp knives and scissors are safer and easier to use than dull ones.

10. To prevent spills, put the covers back on containers tightly. If you do spill, clean it up right away.

11. If your craft doesn't turn out exactly like the picture in the book, that's terrific! The pictures are there just to give you ideas. Crafts become more meaningful when you add your own personal touch.

12. Cleanup is part of making crafts, too. Leave your work area as clean as you found it. Wash and dry dishes, trays, and tabletops. Sweep the floor. Throw away the garbage.

THREADING A NEEDLE

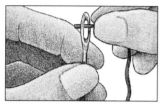

1. Wet the tip of the thread in your mouth. Then push the tip of the thread through the eye of the needle.

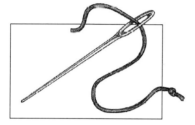

2. Pull about 5 inches of the thread through the needle. Then tie a double knot near the end of the long tail of thread.

LETTER PERFECT

Beautiful handwriting was important in Felicity's time. Some people thought making words look beautiful was more important than spelling them right! In 1774, the most popular writing tool used by both children and adults was the quill pen.

The quill pen was usually made from a turkey or goose feather. One colonial writing book said, "Feathers from the left wing fit the right hand best." To make a quill pen, an adult used a penknife to cut a *nib*, or sharp writing point, at the end of the feather. Children usually weren't allowed to make their own pens until they were 12 years old.

To use a quill pen, a writer dipped the nib into ink. Liquid ink was not available in stores. Families usually made their own ink from powders. They also made ink from berries and walnut shells.

Sometimes colonial children practiced penmanship in copybooks they made by sewing sheets of paper together. Felicity tried to practice her penmanship in her copybook, but often she ended up drawing pictures of horses instead!

Children and adults wrote in diaries, too, which they sometimes called *monitors*. They wrote about what the weather was like and what they did each day, but they hardly ever wrote about what they thought or felt. People also kept blank books called *commonplace books*. In these books, they wrote down memorable words or phrases from books they read or speeches they heard. Children wrote down riddles and words to their favorite songs in their commonplace books.

People wrote lots of letters in Felicity's time, too. That was the only way to communicate with loved ones who lived far away. Traveling was slow and difficult on bumpy dirt roads, and there were no telephones in 1774!

LETTER PERFECT

Quill Pen

•

Berry Ink

•

Walnut Ink

•

Wax Seal

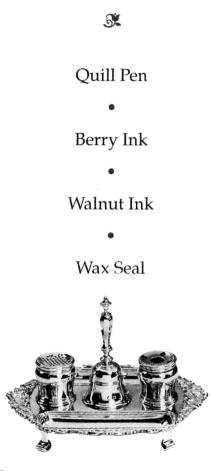

INKSTANDS

Inkstands similar to this one, also called **standishes**, *were used by some wealthy colonists. Most inkstands held an ink pot and a pounce pot.* **Pounce** *was a powder made from ground-up cuttlefish bones. Colonists sprinkled pounce on their writing to help the ink dry. Some inkstands also held a bell. When a writer rang the bell, a servant came to mail the finished letter.*

Pages from a colonial girl's diary.

QUILL PEN

In 1774, quill pens were made from
the wing feathers of large birds,
such as geese and turkeys.

MATERIALS

Goose quill or any other good-sized feather,
   about 10 inches long*
Small knife or scissors
Cutting board
Straight pin
Ink (*See pages 8 and 9 to make your own.*)
Piece of felt, 5 inches square
Writing paper
Available at craft stores or at poultry farms.

DIRECTIONS

1. Let the quill soak in warm, soapy water for
15 minutes.

2. Ask an adult to help you trim off 2 inches of
the bottom feathers of the quill.

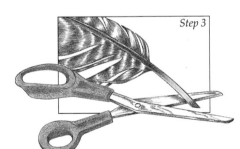

Step 3

3. Cut off the end of the quill stalk at an angle.
This will be the point, or *nib*, of your quill pen.

4. Use a straight pin to clean out the inside of the
stalk. Work carefully so you don't crack the nib.

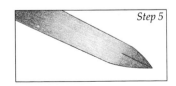

Step 5

5. Now cut a small slit in the nib. This slit will help
control the ink flow.

6. Dip the nib of the quill pen into the ink.
Press the nib gently onto the felt to blot the
excess ink.

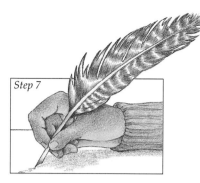

Step 7

7. Hold your pen at a slant to practice writing. Experiment by holding the pen at different angles and using different amounts of pressure.

8. When your quill pen runs dry, dip the nib into the ink again, blot the excess ink onto the felt, and continue writing.

9. If the nib wears down, follow steps 3 through 5 to cut another one. Your pen will be new again.

10. When you have gotten used to using the quill pen, try practicing the fancy letters and numbers shown on page 42. 🖋

WRITING THE DECLARATION OF INDEPENDENCE

Thomas Jefferson used this portable desk to write a draft of the Declaration of Independence, a document that explained why the colonists wanted to be independent from England. When the draft of the Declaration was complete, a man named Timothy Matlack copied it neatly onto **parchment,** *an animal skin specially prepared to be used as paper.*

BERRY INK

Try making this ink with one kind of berry, or mix and match berries to make your own special ink!

MATERIALS

Measuring cup and spoon
1 cup ripe berries, such as raspberries, strawberries, or blackberries
Strainer
Small jar with lid
Spoon
1 teaspoon vinegar
1 teaspoon salt
Red or blue food coloring *(optional)*

DIRECTIONS

1. Place a few berries into the strainer. Hold the strainer over the small jar.

2. Use the back of the spoon to crush the berries so that the juice drips into the jar.

3. Empty the strainer. Continue crushing the berries a few at a time until they've all been squeezed into juice.

4. Add the vinegar and salt to the berry juice and stir until the salt dissolves.

5. If the ink is too pale, add a drop of red or blue food coloring.

6. Berry ink spoils quickly, so make only a little at a time. Keep the ink jar tightly covered when you're not using it. ❧

Step 2

WRITING MASTERS

In colonial times, writing masters were honored in the colonies. They taught penmanship and copied important documents, business statements, and invitations.

WALNUT INK

MATERIALS

Shells from 8 walnuts
Clean kitchen towel
Hammer
Small saucepan
Measuring cup and spoon
1 cup water
Strainer
Small jar with lid
$\frac{1}{2}$ teaspoon vinegar
$\frac{1}{2}$ teaspoon salt

*Make your own beautiful brown
ink just as Felicity did.*

DIRECTIONS

1. Wrap the shells in the towel. Have an adult help you use the hammer to crush them.

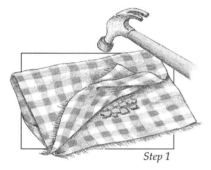

Step 1

2. Put the crushed shells into the saucepan and add the water.

3. Heat the water until it *boils*, or bubbles rapidly. Then turn down the heat and let the water *simmer*, or bubble gently, for 45 minutes. The water will turn dark brown.

4. When the mixture has finished simmering, let it cool for 15 minutes. Then have an adult help you pour it through a strainer into a small jar.

5. Add the vinegar and salt to the walnut ink and stir until the salt dissolves.

6. Keep the ink jar tightly covered when you're not using it. Otherwise, your ink will dry out! 🖋

INK FROM SOOT?

Soot from the inside of chimneys and lamps mixed with water made a good black ink. Colonists made beautiful inks from other natural ingredients, too. Berries made shades of red and purple, and nutshells, roots, and tree bark made rich, dark browns.

WAX SEAL

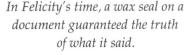

In Felicity's time, a wax seal on a document guaranteed the truth of what it said.

MATERIALS

Sheet of practice paper
Matches or lighter
Sealing wax or tapered candle
Signet, or seal, for making impressions in wax*
Available in stationery stores, or see the next page to make your own.

DIRECTIONS

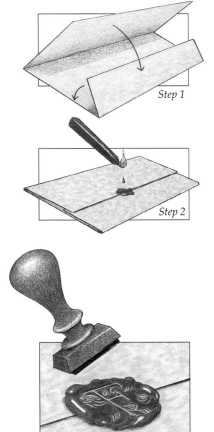

Step 1

Step 2

Step 4

1. Spread a sheet of practice paper on a table. Fold it as shown. Have an adult help you light the wick on the sealing wax or candle.

2. Hold the sealing wax or candle at an angle over the place where you want to make your seal. Let the wax drip onto that spot.

3. When the size of the wax spot matches the size of your signet, blow out the flame. Press the design end of your signet into the wax. Don't press too long, or the wax will harden.

4. Lift the signet. If the seal is too faint or off-center, "erase" it. Drip more wax on top and press your signet into the wax again.

WAFER CONTAINERS

*The center container on this inkstand held **sealing wafers.** Colonists used thin wafers made of flour mixed with gum or gelatin for sealing their everyday letters. They folded a letter, moistened a wafer, and pressed the wafer onto the letter to seal it.*

SEALING LETTERS

*In Felicity's time, envelopes didn't have glue you could lick. Instead, people used wax to seal their important documents. Merchants sold sticks of sealing wax in two colors—red and black. Colonists usually used red sealing wax. They used black sealing wax only when they were in **mourning**, or grieving over someone's death.*

MAKE YOUR OWN SIGNET

MATERIALS
Sheet of paper
Pencil
Self-hardening clay
Ruler
Paper towel
Vegetable oil

DIRECTIONS

1. Plan a simple design on paper. If you use your initials, make sure to draw them backward.

2. Form a clay rectangle about 2 inches long, 1 inch wide, and 1 inch tall. Draw your design into 1 end of the rectangle. Then carve away the clay around the design so the design "stands up" from the clay rectangle. Let the clay harden overnight.

3. Use a paper towel to oil the design each time you use it so the wax won't stick to the clay.

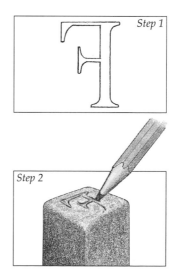

Step 1

Step 2

FUN AND GAMES

The Magazine in Williamsburg.

Felicity and Elizabeth sometimes played on the green next to the *Magazine,* where the colonists kept their gunpowder and other supplies. The green was a wide, open grassy place in the middle of Williamsburg. When soldiers weren't marching there, the green was a perfect place for Felicity and Elizabeth to fly a kite.

When they finished tying on bits of paper for the tail, they both held onto the kite line and slowly let the wind take the kite higher and higher. They were careful not to let the kite get tangled in a tree branch, but they didn't have to worry about electrical wires or telephone lines. There weren't any in 1774!

On Grandfather's plantation, Felicity might have played a game of *bowls* on the bowling green. This isn't at all like the kind of bowling people do today. To play, a white ball called a *jack* was rolled onto the green. It became the target. Then each player tossed a ball called a *bowl*, trying to roll it as close to the jack as possible. That was tricky to do. The bowls couldn't be rolled in a straight line because they were weighted on one side. To make it even harder, bowling greens usually weren't level.

Some games and toys haven't changed much at all since colonial times. In the 1700s, children played with dolls, dollhouses, marbles, tops, tea services, balls, and whistles. They also played games like tag and hopscotch, which was called "Scotch-hoppers" in Felicity's time.

Wooden tops from the 1700s.

In the winter, boys and girls loved *coasting*, or sledding. At first, the word "coasting" meant being lazy or idle, but then it came to mean sledding downhill. Children thought coasting was great fun, but some adults thought it was too dangerous!

FUN AND GAMES

✣

Game of Graces

•

Cup and Ball

•

Kite

CUP AND BALL

*This girl is playing with a cup and ball. The toy was also called a **bilbo-catcher**, an English way of saying the French word **bilboquet** (BILL-bo-kay). In old French, **bille** means "ball" and **bocquet** means "the point of a spear." Some bilbo-catchers had a stick in place of the cup. There was a hole in the ball, and a player caught the ball on the stick.*

GAME OF GRACES

Felicity tried to hold a graceful pose each time she tossed or caught a hoop!

MATERIALS

Foam paintbrush, 1 inch wide
Acrylic paint, any color
4 wooden dowels, each $\frac{1}{2}$ inch wide and 2 feet long
2 wooden hoops, each 10 inches wide*
8 ribbons, each $\frac{1}{4}$ inch wide and 6 feet long
Scissors
The inner rings of large embroidery hoops work well.

DIRECTIONS

1. Paint the dowels and then set them aside to dry. They will be your game wands.

2. To decorate a hoop, tie an end of a ribbon around the hoop in a double knot.

3. Have an adult help you wrap the ribbon all the way around the hoop. Leave about an inch between each wrap.

4. When you reach the place where you started wrapping, tie the ends of the ribbon together in a double knot. Cut off the short tail of ribbon close to the knot. Let the rest of the ribbon hang down as a streamer.

5. Tie another ribbon a quarter of the way around the hoop as shown.

6. Wrap the second ribbon all the way around the hoop, close to the first ribbon. Then tie the ends of this ribbon together, just as you did in step 4.

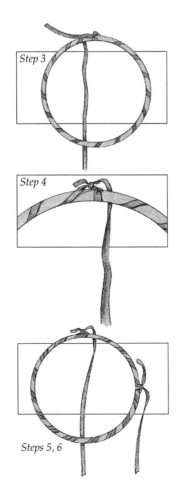

Step 3

Step 4

Steps 5, 6

7. Repeat steps 5 and 6 to tie on 2 more ribbons. You will end up with 4 equally spaced streamers hanging from your hoop.

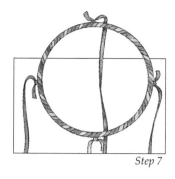

Step 7

8. Decorate the second hoop with ribbons in the same way.

9. To play, you'll need a partner. You each get 1 hoop and 2 wands. Stand about 10 feet away from your partner.

10. Try the game with 1 hoop first. Cross your wands in front of you, with the hoop resting where the wands cross.

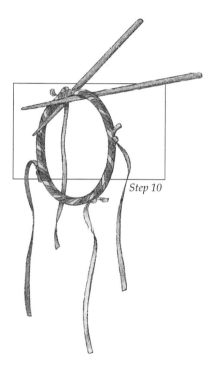

Step 10

11. Toss the hoop back and forth with your partner. The object of the game is to toss the hoop back and forth as quickly as possible without dropping it.

12. When you've mastered 1 hoop, try tossing 2 hoops back and forth at the same time! 🌸

THE THREE GRACES

Some people think the Game of Graces got its name from the Graces in Greek myths. The Graces were three goddesses who gave beauty and grace to girls. In 1774, girls were supposed to be graceful in everything they did. They weren't even supposed to play instruments like the French horn because puffing out their cheeks was considered very ungraceful!

CUP AND BALL

*It takes practice to swing the ball
and catch it in the cup!*

MATERIALS

Small artist's paintbrush
Acrylic paints, any colors
Unfinished wooden wall peg, 3½ inches long
Small unfinished wooden cup*
Unfinished wooden bead
Wood glue
Piece of cotton cord, 18 inches long
Scissors
*If you can't find a small wooden cup at a craft store,
 try using half a walnut shell instead.*

DIRECTIONS

Step 2

Step 3

Step 4

1. Paint the peg, cup, and bead any colors you like.

2. After the paint has dried, glue the wooden cup to the flat end of the peg. Let the glue dry overnight.

3. Tie 3 or 4 knots near 1 end of the cord. Then slip the wooden bead onto the cord. Cut off the short tail of cord close to the knot.

4. Tie the other end of the cord tightly around the peg, about ¼ inch below the cup. Cut off the extra cord close to the knot.

5. To play with your cup and ball, hold the peg and let the ball hang down.

6. Then swing the ball into the air and try to catch it in the cup! ✖

KITE

MATERIALS

2-foot wooden dowel, $\frac{1}{4}$ inch wide
3-foot wooden dowel, $\frac{1}{4}$ inch wide
Scissors
Ruler
Large ball of string
White glue
Small knife
Sheet of lightweight paper, 3 feet square
20 strips of colored paper, each 2 by 3 inches
1-foot wooden dowel, $\frac{1}{2}$ inch wide

*Kites are a way to touch the sky with
your feet still on the ground!*

DIRECTIONS

1. Form a cross with the 2-foot and 3-foot dowels. Cut a 3-foot piece of string and tie 1 end tightly around the 3-foot dowel as shown.

2. With a partner, wind the string crossways a few times in 1 direction, and then in the other. Stop winding when there are 3 inches left.

3. Wrap the string loosely around the 3-foot dowel once, and then tie it in a tight double knot. Squeeze a little glue onto the knot to help hold it in place.

4. Ask an adult to make a notch at the end of each dowel with a knife—a total of 4 notches.

5. Cut an 8-foot piece of string and tie a double knot at the end. Slip the string into the top notch and pull it tight. ➡

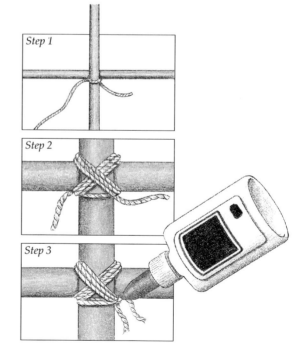

Step 1

Step 2

Step 3

Step 5

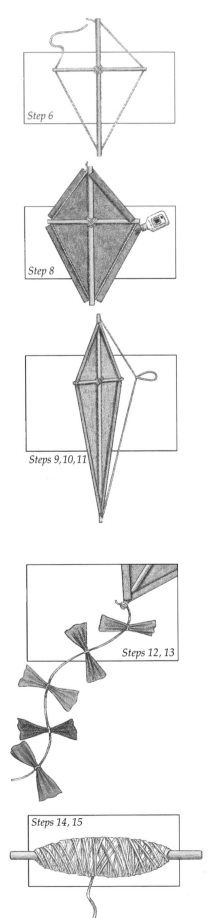

Step 6

Step 8

Steps 9, 10, 11

Steps 12, 13

Steps 14, 15

6. Wind the string tightly around the kite frame, slipping the string into each notch. Tie the ends of the string together in a double knot. Cut off the extra string.

7. Lay the kite frame on the paper. Cut the paper about 1 inch larger than the kite frame.

8. Cut away the corners of the paper, as shown. Then fold the edges of the paper over the string and glue them down.

9. Now make a *bridle* to guide your kite as it flies. Cut a 5-foot piece of string and tie 1 end around the top of the kite frame in a double knot.

10. Ask an adult to help you tie a loop in the string about 1$\frac{1}{2}$ feet down from the top.

11. Tie the other end of the string around the bottom of the frame, and cut off the extra string.

12. To make a tail, cut a 10-foot piece of string. Tie paper strips onto the string, about 6 inches apart.

13. When you have finished, tie 1 end of the tail string to the bottom of the kite.

14. To make the kite line, cut a 30-foot piece of string and tie 1 end around the center of the 1-foot dowel.

15. Wind the string around the dowel until there are 6 inches left. Leave room at each end of the dowel so you can hold onto it.

16. Tie the end of the string to the loop on the bridle. Go fly your kite! 🪁

Step 16

KITES AND ELECTRICITY

In 1752, Benjamin Franklin attached a metal wire to a homemade kite and tied a metal key to the kite line. Then he flew the kite in a lightning storm. Lightning struck the metal wire on the kite and traveled down the wet kite line. When it reached the key, it made a spark. The spark proved that lightning in the sky was electricity!

ON THE PLANTATION

Summers in Williamsburg were steamy hot. Felicity and her family escaped the heat of the city by visiting Grandfather's plantation each summer. One of Felicity's favorite places on the plantation was the bank of the wide York River. She loved to sit at the river's edge and dangle her toes in the cool water. During the hottest part of the day, Felicity sat in the shade of the garden, picking flowers to trim her wide-brimmed straw hat. If there were no breezes, she used a hand-held fan to cool herself.

Summer on the plantation was pleasant and carefree for well-to-do families. Children played games on the wide, green lawn around the great house. Some plantations had herds of tame deer, and children often made pets of the fawns. And every plantation had horses to ride!

Families often gathered at the river's edge to have a fish feast. Men and boys fished in the morning, and then everyone ate the fish for dinner. Oftentimes many families came to a fish feast, and each family brought food to share. Sometimes there were boat races in the afternoon and music and dancing in the evening.

This carefree life would not have been possible without the hard work of slaves. During much of the year, most people in slavery worked in the fields from sunup to sundown, planting, tending, and harvesting crops like tobacco, corn, and wheat. Other slaves worked as cooks, maids, carpenters, blacksmiths, shoemakers, spinners, weavers, and knitters. Together they provided almost everything the plantation needed, doing all the jobs that made life comfortable for the plantation owner and his family.

ON THE PLANTATION

Folding Fan

•

Fancy Straw Hat

•

Fruit Pyramid

From the book Felicity Saves the Day

PLANTATION LIFE

Living on a plantation was a lot like living in a little village. A plantation often included gardens full of fruits and vegetables to eat, stables of horses to ride, craftspeople to make things like furniture and clothing, and even docks on the river for shipping tobacco and receiving visitors.

FOLDING FAN

A delicate fan was the perfect finishing touch for a colonial girl's outfit.

MATERIALS

Pencil
Sheet of tracing paper
Sheet of newspaper
2 sheets of poster board, each 10 by 14 inches
Scissors
Foam paintbrush, 1 inch wide
Acrylic paints, any colors
Ruler
Sharp knife or craft knife
Nutpick *(optional)*
Cutting board
Brass fastener
3-foot piece of ribbon, $1/4$ inch wide
White glue
Small artist's paintbrush

DIRECTIONS

1. Use a pencil to trace the fan blade pattern shown on page 43 onto tracing paper. Don't cut it out.

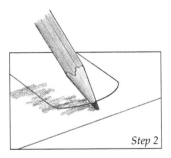

Step 2

2. Place the sheet of tracing paper onto the newspaper, design side down. Use the side of the pencil to color over the back of the pattern.

3. Place the tracing paper on top of 1 of the sheets of poster board, design side up. Then draw over the lines of the pattern, pressing firmly.

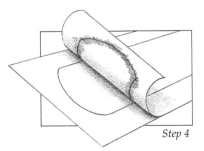

Step 4

4. Lift up the tracing paper. The pencil markings will come off where you traced. Cut out the fan blade. Use it as a pattern to trace 11 more fan blades onto the poster board, for a total of 12 blades. Then cut them out.

5. Use the foam paintbrush to give the blades a base coat of paint. Paint 1 side of each blade. Let them dry, and then paint the other sides.

6. When the paint is dry, use the pencil and ruler to mark a dot in the center of each blade, $\frac{1}{4}$ inch from the bottom. Have an adult help you use the knife or nutpick to poke a hole through each dot.

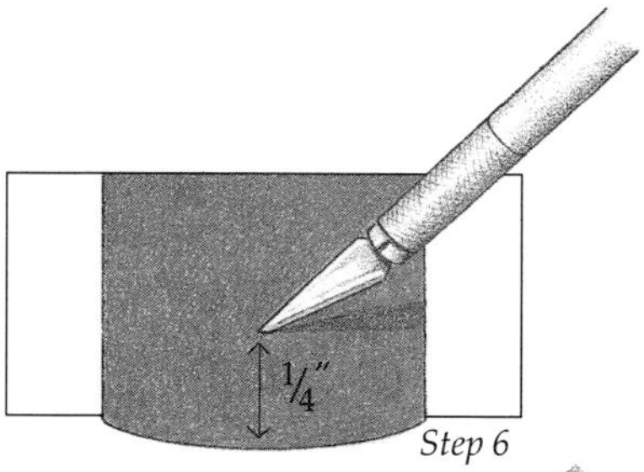

Step 6

7. Starting 1 inch from the top of each blade, draw a 1-inch line down the center. Have an adult help you use the knife to cut on each line.

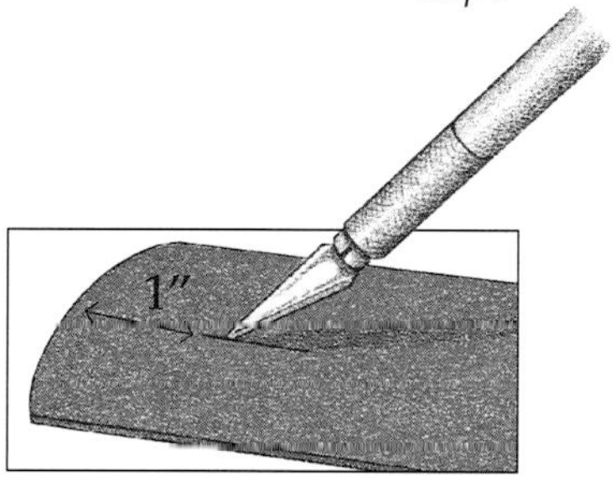

Step 7

8. Stack the blades together. Push the brass fastener through the holes at the bottoms of the blades. Fasten it, and then spread out the fan.

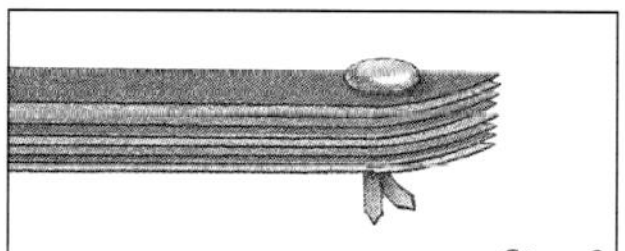
Step 8

9. Tie a double knot at the end of the ribbon. Then, starting at the back side of the fan, push the ribbon through the slit at the top of the first blade. Pull the ribbon through until the knot catches.

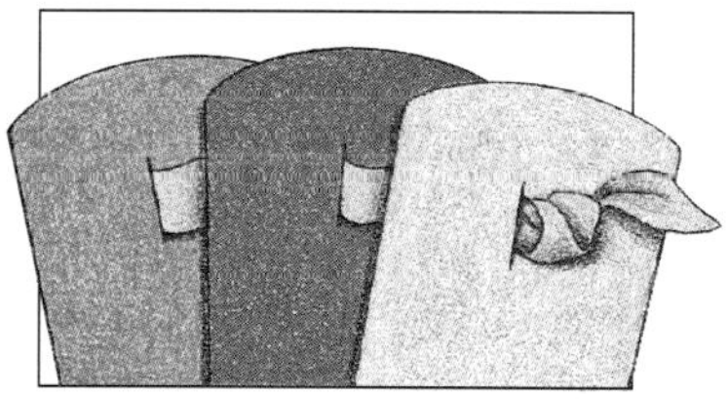
Steps 9, 10

10. Weave the ribbon through the rest of the slits. When you've finished, arrange the blades until they are evenly spaced.

11. Wrap the ribbon around the back of the last blade. Glue it in place. Cut off the extra ribbon. For a finishing touch, use the artist's paintbrush to decorate each blade.

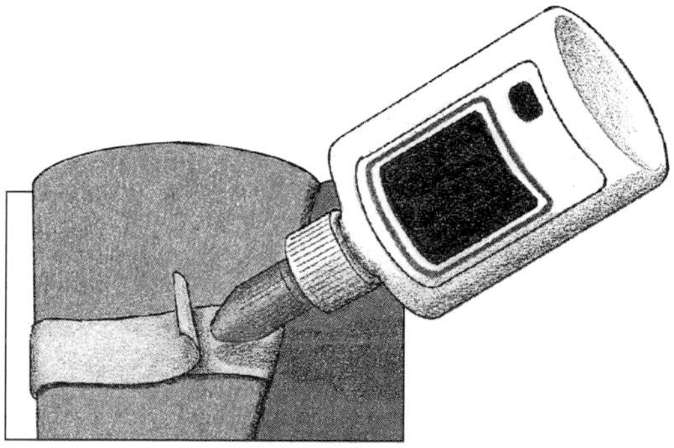
Step 11

FANCY STRAW HAT

Make a beautiful bonnet to shade your face from the hot summer sun.

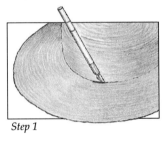

Step 1

MATERIALS

Sharp knife or craft knife
Cutting board
Ruler
Straw hat
5-foot piece of satin ribbon, 2 inches wide
Scissors
Any of the following: silk flowers, colorful feathers, and extra ribbon for bows
Fabric glue
Paper towels

DIRECTIONS

1. Have an adult help you use the knife to cut a 1-inch slit where the crown of the hat meets the brim.

2. Cut another 1-inch slit on the opposite side of the hat.

3. Starting on the underside of the hat, thread the ribbon through 1 of the slits.

4. Then pull the ribbon over the crown of the hat and thread it through the other slit.

5. Keep pulling the ribbon through the slits until you have the same length of ribbon on both sides. Then cut the ribbon ends at a slant.

6. If you're using silk flowers, cut off the stems just below the blossoms.

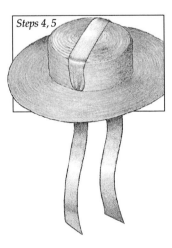

Steps 4, 5

7. Plan your hat design. Decide what kinds and colors of flowers, feathers, and ribbons you like best. Then arrange them on your hat to see what looks best together.

8. When you're happy with your hat design, glue on your decorations. If any glue seeps through the straw, wipe it off with a paper towel.

9. After the glue has dried, your hat is ready to wear. Tie the ribbon ends under your chin, and you're all set for a stroll through the garden! 🐛

WEAVING RIBBONS

*This woman is weaving decorative **tapes**, or ribbons, by hand. Colonial girls and women used these tapes on their hats, in their hair, as shoelaces, and as garters to keep their stockings up.*

KEEPING HOUSES COOL

There were no electric fans or air conditioners in 1774. To keep their houses cool, colonists put blinds or shutters on their windows to keep out the hot sun. During the hottest weather, some people spent all their time outdoors on their covered porches and in the shade of trees. They only went inside to sleep!

FRUIT PYRAMID

Felicity made pyramids from fruit grown on Grandfather's plantation.

MATERIALS

Knife
Styrofoam® cone, about 1 foot tall*
Ruler
Dinner plate
20 apples
20 toothpicks
Small herb sprigs or evergreen boughs
Large leaves to decorate base of pyramid
Available in craft stores or florists' shops.

Step 1

DIRECTIONS

1. If the top of your cone is not flat, have an adult help you use the knife to cut off an inch from the point of the cone.

2. Place the cone in the middle of a dinner plate. Set the plate aside.

3. Sort your apples by size. Use the bigger apples for the bottom of your fruit pyramid and the smaller apples for the top.

4. Push a toothpick halfway into 1 of the bigger apples.

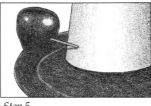

Step 5

5. Then push the toothpick into the cone, near the bottom.

6. Place the second apple next to the first apple and attach it to the cone in the same way.

7. Continue placing apples around the bottom of the cone until you've made a complete circle.

8. Then make a second circle of apples above the first circle. Continue covering the sides of the cone with more apples in the same way.

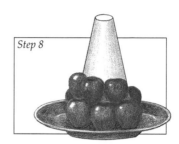

Step 8

9. For the top of the cone, push a toothpick halfway into the bottom of 1 of the small apples. Then push the toothpick into the flat top of the cone.

10. Use small herb sprigs or evergreen boughs to fill in the spaces between the apples. Then arrange large leaves around the bottom of the pyramid.

Step 10

11. You can make pyramids with other fruits, too, like oranges, lemons, and limes. Mix and match! 🌺

DECORATING THE TABLE

In colonial times, decorating the dinner table was an art. Women and girls made pyramids of fruits and sweets to add height and color to the table. It was also important for the table to look balanced. If there was a round dish on one side of the table, there had to be a round dish on the other side of the table, too, for balance.

A Stitch in Time

Learning to sew was important for girls and women in colonial times. Felicity helped her mother mend the family's clothes. There were no sewing machines in Felicity's day, so she and her mother had to do all their sewing by hand. That could take hours each day—there were holes to darn, hems to move up or down, and seams to take in or let out. Sometimes Felicity thought she'd never be free from those miles and miles of stitches!

Colonial girls learned fancy sewing, too. Felicity and Elizabeth practiced their stitchery each afternoon at their lessons with Miss Manderly. They worked on their samplers of stitches, and they made other projects like embroidered pincushions. In Felicity's day, pincushions were popular baby gifts. Colonists hung pincushions that said "Welcome Little Stranger" on the front doors of families with newborn babies. Women and girls also decorated their petticoats with beautiful embroidery. Sometimes they even stitched verses from the Bible along the edges of their gowns.

Fancy stitchery on a colonial petticoat.

During the Revolutionary War, England stopped sending things like cloth to the colonies. So women often wove their own cloth, called *homespun*, from cotton, linen, or wool thread. Farmers grew cotton and *flax*, the plant used to make linen, and many colonists raised sheep. Some patriots agreed not to butcher their sheep during the war. They wanted to shear the sheep's wool year after year so they could have as much wool as possible for clothing.

In 1775, patriotic women made 13,000 warm wool coats for soldiers. Each coat had a label with the name of the woman who sewed it and the town where she lived. Today, the list of the group of soldiers who wore those coats is still known as the "Coat Roll."

A STITCH IN TIME

❧

Cross-Stitch Sampler

•

Sachet

•

Friendship Pincushion

SAMPLERS

Almost every colonial girl completed a sampler of stitches to show her fine needlework. But samplers taught more than just stitches. Most samplers included the alphabet and numbers, or verses like this one:

> *This is my sampler,*
> *Here you see,*
> *What care my Mother*
> *Took of me.*

CROSS-STITCH SAMPLER

Frame your sampler so everyone can admire your fine stitches!

MATERIALS

Masking tape
11-count cross-stitch cloth, 10 by 12 inches
Ruler
Fabric pen or pencil
Embroidery hoop, 6 inches wide
Scissors
Embroidery floss *(blue, rose, green)*
Large-eyed embroidery needle
Picture frame, 8 by 10 inches

DIRECTIONS

1. Tape the edges of the cloth so they won't unravel while you work.

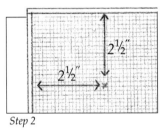

Step 2

2. Lay the fabric on a table. At the upper left corner, measure $2\frac{1}{2}$ inches in from the side and $2\frac{1}{2}$ inches down from the top. Mark a small "x" on that square. This will be the top left stitch of the letter "a."

3. Follow the pattern on page 44 to fill in the rest of the design. Each square on the pattern equals 1 square on the cross-stitch cloth. Count carefully!

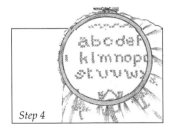

Step 4

4. Take the embroidery hoop apart by loosening the screw. Then place the fabric over the inner hoop so that the top left part of the pattern is inside the hoop. Snap the outer hoop over the fabric and inner hoop, and then tighten the screw.

5. Begin by stitching the top border. Cut an 18-inch piece of blue floss.

6. The floss is made up of 6 strands. To cross-stitch, separate 2 strands.

7. Thread the needle with those 2 strands. Tie a double knot near the other end of the floss.

8. To cross-stitch, come up at A and go down at B.

9. Then come up at C and go down at D. Keep stitching!

10. If you are making several stitches in a row, you can make half of all the stitches first, and then go back and "cross" them.

11. When you near the end of your floss, turn to the back of the cloth and slip the needle under 4 stitches. Cut off the extra floss.

12. Cross-stitch the rest of your design, moving the embroidery hoop as necessary. Use rose for the letters and numbers, green for the trees, and blue for the house and borders.

13. When your design is complete, remove the embroidery hoop. Your sampler is finished and ready for framing! 🌸

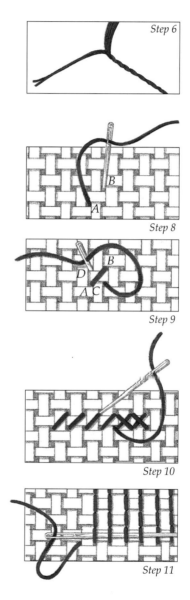

Step 6

Step 8

Step 9

Step 10

Step 11

SACHET

Tuck a sweet-smelling sachet into a dresser drawer to scent your clothes.

MATERIALS

2 pieces of fabric, each 3 by 4 inches
Straight pins
Scissors
Ruler
Thread
Sewing needle
Spoon
Potpourri
Piece of ribbon, 5 inches long

DIRECTIONS

1. Lay 1 piece of fabric on a table with the *right side*, or front side, facing up.

2. Then lay the other piece of fabric on top, with the *wrong side*, or back side, facing up.

3. Use straight pins to pin the pieces of fabric together on 3 sides.

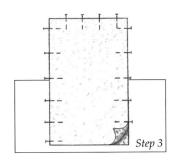

4. Cut an 18-inch piece of thread, and then thread the needle. Tie a double knot near the other end of the thread.

5. Backstitch along the 3 pinned sides, ¼ inch from the edge. To backstitch, come up at A and then go down at B.

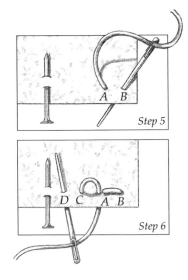

6. Come up at C. Then go down at A and come up at D. Keep stitching!

7. When you finish, tie a knot under the fabric close to your last stitch. Cut off the extra thread.

8. Unpin the fabric and turn the bag inside out. Fill it ¼ full with potpourri.

9. Tuck the fabric's raw edge inside the sachet about 2 inches. Tie the sachet closed with ribbon, and it's finished! 🌺

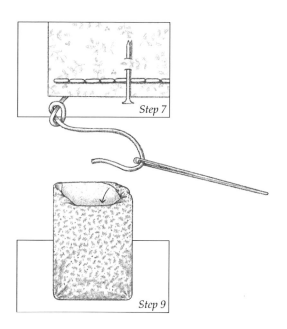

Step 7

Step 9

WASHING DAY

There were no electric washing machines in Felicity's time. Instead, people washed their clothes in large wooden tubs. Water had to be hauled from a well and boiled before the clothes were scrubbed with homemade soap on a bumpy **scrubboard***. Colonists used a* **lifting fork** *to remove the clean clothes from the tub of hot water. Between washings, colonists tucked sachets into trunks and wardrobes to keep clothes smelling fresh.*

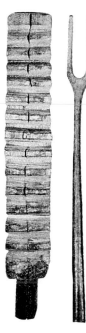

FRIENDSHIP PINCUSHION

Stitch a pincushion for a favorite friend!

MATERIALS

2 pieces of solid-colored fabric, each 4 by 6 inches
Ruler
Fabric pen with disappearing ink
Embroidery hoop, 4 inches wide
Scissors
Embroidery floss, any colors
Embroidery needle
Straight pins
Sewing needle
Thread
Cotton balls
4 tassels *(optional)*

DIRECTIONS

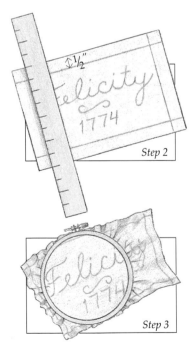

Step 2

Step 3

Step 4

1. Lay both pieces of fabric on a table, with the *right sides*, or front sides, facing up.

2. Use the ruler and fabric pen to draw a line ¹/₂ inch from each edge of both pieces of fabric. Write your name and the year in the center of 1 piece of fabric, inside the lines. If you make a mistake, just let the ink disappear and try again!

3. Take the embroidery hoop apart by loosening the screw. Then place 1 piece of fabric over the inner hoop so that your design is in the middle. Snap the outer hoop over the fabric and inner hoop, and then tighten the screw.

4. Cut an 18-inch piece of embroidery floss. The floss is made up of 6 strands. To embroider, separate 2 strands.

5. Thread the embroidery needle with those 2 strands. Tie a double knot near the other end of the floss.

6. Backstitch your design. To backstitch, come up at A and go down at B.

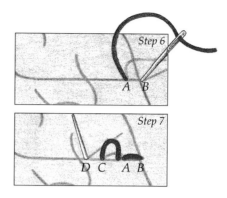

7. Come up at C. Then go down at A and come up at D. Keep stitching!

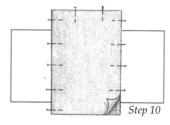

8. When you near the end of your thread, tie a knot under the fabric close to your last stitch. Cut off the extra thread.

9. When you finish stitching, remove the embroidery hoop. Then stitch your friend's name on the other piece of fabric in the same way.

10. Then lay 1 piece of fabric on top of the other, right sides together. Pin 3 edges together. Use the sewing needle and thread to backstitch these 3 sides, ¼ inch from each edge.

Step 10

11. Unpin the fabric and turn it right side out. Stuff the pincushion with cotton balls until it's plump.

12. Tuck the raw edges of fabric inside the pincushion. Pin the edges together and sew the fourth side closed.

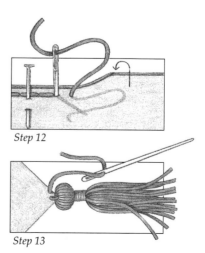

Step 12

13. Remove the pins. If you like, finish your pincushion by sewing colorful tassels on the corners. 🪡

Step 13

SWEET SCENTS

A Williamsburg garden.

nglish colonists wanted their gardens in
Virginia to look like the gardens they had
known in England. Some colonists even
brought seeds, bulbs, roots, and cuttings from their
favorite flowers with them on their long voyage
from England. They planted hollyhocks, English
roses, carnations, sweet William, and many other
English flowers in their Virginia gardens to remind
them of home.

For half the year, Virginia sizzles with heat.
Most colonial gardens had shade trees, and many

gardens had vine-covered *arbors,* or shaded walkways. Colonists grew fragrant fruit trees, such as apple, pear, apricot, cherry, and plum. Tropical fruits like oranges usually came from the West Indies, although a few wealthy colonists had hothouses for growing them.

Felicity's favorite place to be was in her garden. She loved planting her flowers, vegetables, and herbs in straight, tidy rows. She brought her garden indoors, too. In the spring and summer, she displayed cut flowers on the mantel in vases and jars, which were also called *posy-holders.* She also made small bouquets called *tussie-mussies.* In colonial times, tussie-mussies were popular as decorations for weddings, and people sometimes placed them on a table to freshen a room.

Drying flowers and plants was considered an art in Felicity's day. In the fall, Felicity dried flowers, pods, and leaves for winter bouquets, and she used dried petals to make *potpourri.* Colonists sometimes grew flowers like hyacinths in their homes over the winter, too. But often the cold killed the flowers anyway. One woman wrote in her diary that it got so cold her flowers froze in the front parlor!

A colonial family in their garden.

SWEET SCENTS

Potpourri

•

Tussie-Mussie

•

Pomander Ball

BELL GLASSES

*Colonists sometimes put bell-shaped glass domes, called **bell glasses,** over plants and flowers to help them grow faster. Bell glasses acted as mini-greenhouses. One colonist said bell glasses looked like "beehives of glass, very curious."*

POTPOURRI

Leave potpourri in a bowl to give a room a fresh scent.

MATERIALS

Measuring cup and spoon
4 cups flower petals
2 cups herb leaves
Cookie sheet
Mixing spoon
Glass jar with lid
6 tablespoons each of ground cinnamon,
    nutmeg, allspice, and whole cloves
Scented oil

DIRECTIONS

1. Spread your flower petals and herb leaves on the cookie sheet and let them dry for about 1 week. Stir them each day to help them dry faster.

2. When you can crumble the petals and leaves between your fingers, they're ready to make into potpourri.

3. Put 1/2 inch of dried petals and leaves into the jar. Then sprinkle them with 1 tablespoon each of cinnamon, nutmeg, allspice, and cloves.

4. Keep adding layers of dried plants and spices until the jar is almost full. Add a few drops of scented oil on top.

5. Cover the jar tightly. Store it in a cool, dark place for 1 week. Stir the potpourri every 2 or 3 days. Use your potpourri to make the sachet on page 32!

ROSY-CAKES

Colonial children sometimes made dainty "rosy-cakes" by sprinkling sugar and cinnamon on rose petals. They gave the sugary petals as treats to their favorite friends to eat.

TUSSIE-MUSSIE

MATERIALS

Scissors
1 rose
Ruler
Fresh herb sprigs, such as basil, thyme, sage,
  and rosemary*
String
Lace doily or hankie
2 ribbons, each 1 foot long
Available in grocery stores or at farmers' markets.

*Tussie-mussies make perfect flower-girl
and bridesmaid bouquets.*

DIRECTIONS

1. Cut the stem of the rose to 4 inches. Then cut
   the stems of the herb sprigs to 3 inches. Cut off
   a few leaves at the bottom of each plant to leave
   1/2 inch of bare stem.

2. Arrange the smallest herb sprigs around the
   rose. Keep adding herb sprigs around the rose,
   working from the smallest sprigs to the largest.

Step 2

3. Tie the string in a double knot around the
   stems of the plants. Cut off the extra string.

Step 3

4. Wrap the lace doily or hankie around the
   stems. Then tie it in place with colorful
   ribbons. ❧

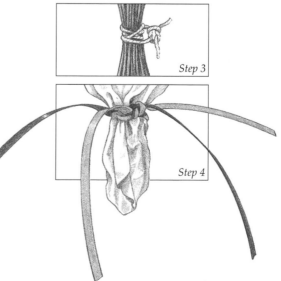

Step 4

ROSE WATER

*Boiled rose petals made **rose water**,
which was used by colonists as a
perfume, an air freshener, and a
flavoring in cooking.*

POMANDER BALL

Spicy pomander balls make wonderful holiday gifts and decorations.

MATERIALS

1 small orange
Transparent tape
Small nail
1 ounce whole cloves
Small bowl
Measuring spoon
1 tablespoon cinnamon
1 tablespoon nutmeg
1 tablespoon ginger
2 ribbons, each 2 feet long

DIRECTIONS

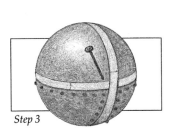

Step 3

1. Starting at the top of the orange, wrap a strip of tape all the way around it.

2. Then wrap a strip of tape around the orange in the other direction.

3. Pomander balls are decorated with cloves. Use a nail to poke holes in the orange along the edges of the tape. Press a clove into each hole.

4. Poke more holes into the orange, but don't fill them with cloves. These holes will hold the spices you'll sprinkle over the orange in step 6.

5. Remove the tape. The ribbon will be wrapped over these tape paths later on.

6. Place the orange into a small bowl and sprinkle it with cinnamon, nutmeg, and ginger. Make sure the spices fill up the empty holes.

7. Leave the pomander in the bowl to dry in a cool, dark closet for about 1 week. As it dries, it will shrink and harden.

8. After it has dried, wrap a ribbon around the orange along 1 of the tape paths. Tie it in a double knot at the top of the orange.

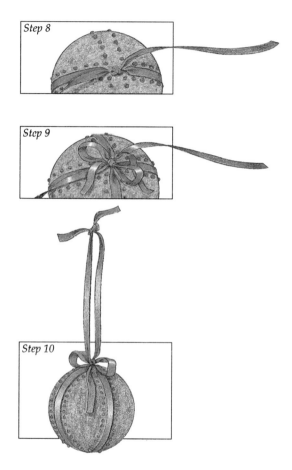

Step 8

Step 9

Step 10

9. Wrap the second ribbon around the orange along the other tape path. Tie it in a double knot at the top of the orange, and then tie it into a bow.

10. Form a loop with the long ribbon tails by tying them together in a double knot.

11. Hang your pomander ball in the kitchen, bathroom, or a closet. Its spicy scent will last for years. ❧

VISITING SICK FRIENDS

When colonists went to visit sick friends, they often carried pomander balls or tussie-mussies with them. They believed that if they smelled the pomander balls or tussie-mussies, they wouldn't get sick themselves.

PATTERNS

A B C D E F G
H I J K L M
N O P Q R S T
U V W X Y Z

abcdefghijklm
nopqrstuvwxyz
1234567890

Fan Blade

SAMPLER

AMERICAN GIRLS PASTIMES™
Activities from the Past for Girls of Today

You'll enjoy all the Pastimes books about your favorite characters in The American Girls Collection®.

Learn to cook foods that Felicity, Kirsten, Addy, Samantha, and Molly loved with the Pastimes **COOKBOOKS.** They're filled with great recipes and fun party ideas.

Make the same crafts that your favorite American Girls character made. Each of the **CRAFT BOOKS** has simple step-by-step instructions and fascinating historical facts.

Imagine that you are your favorite American Girls character as you stage a play about her. Each of the **THEATER KITS** has four Play Scripts and a Director's Guide.

Learn about fashions of the past as you cut out the ten outfits in each of the **PAPER DOLL KITS.** Each kit also contains a make-it-yourself book plus historical fun facts.

There are **CRAFT KITS** for each character with directions and supplies to make 3 crafts from the Pastimes Craft Books. Craft Kits are available only through Pleasant Company's catalogue, which you can request by filling out the postcard below.

Turn the page to learn more about the other delights in The American Girls Collection. ⟶

I'm an American girl who loves to get mail. Please send me a catalogue of The American Girls Collection®:

My name is _____

My address is _____

City_____ State _____ Zip _____

Parent's signature_____

And send a catalogue to my friend:

My friend's name is_____

Address _____

City_____ State _____ Zip _____

THE AMERICAN GIRLS COLLECTION®

The American Girls Collection tells the stories of five lively nine-year-old girls who lived long ago—Felicity, Kirsten, Addy, Samantha, and Molly. You can read about their adventures in a series of beautifully illustrated books of historical fiction. By reading these books, you'll learn what growing up was like in times past.

There is also a lovable doll for each character with beautiful clothes and lots of wonderful accessories. The dolls and their accessories make the stories of the past come alive today for American girls like you.

The American Girls Collection is for you if you love to curl up with a good book. It's for you if you like to play with dolls and act out stories. It's for you if you want something so special that you will treasure it for years to come.

To learn more about The American Girls Collection, fill out the postcard on the other side of the page and mail it to Pleasant Company, or call **1-800-845-0005.** We will send you a free catalogue about all the books, dolls, dresses, and other delights in The American Girls Collection.

NO POSTAGE
NECESSARY
IF MAILED
IN THE
UNITED STATES

BUSINESS REPLY MAIL
First Class Mail   Permit No. 1137   Middleton, WI USA

POSTAGE WILL BE PAID BY ADDRESSEE

PLEASANT COMPANY
P.O. Box 620497
Middleton, WI 53562-9940